real-life stories

LIVING AS A REFUGEE

Mohamed's Story

by Louise Armstrong
Produced in association with
International Institute of St. Louis

WE WOULD LIKE TO THANK THE FOLLOWING FOR THEIR HELP IN THE PRODUCTION OF THIS BOOK:

The Nazari family;
Beth Radtke and Amy De Leal of the International Institute, St. Louis;
Stephanie Cordle for her brilliant photographs of Mohammed;
Jean Coppendale and Indexing Specialists (UK) Ltd;

and our special thanks to

Mohamed

without whom this book would not have been possible.

Copyright © ticktock Entertainment Ltd 2005
First published in Great Britain in 2005 by ticktock Media Ltd,
Unit 2, Orchard Business Centre, North Farm Road, Tunbridge Wells, Kent TN2 3XF
ISBN 1 86007 825 7 pbk
Printed in China
A CIP catalogue record for this book is available from the British Library.

Picture credits (t=top; b=bottom; c=centre; l=left; r=right): Corbis: 4l, 29t, 29b, 40l, 40r, 41, 44t.
Exile Images: 9t, 9b, 11, 44b. International Institute: 39t. Nazari Family: 10t. Stephanie Cordle: 1, 3, 8, 10b, 12, 14, 16, 18, 19l, 22, 34 25l, 25r, 26, 27t, 27b, 28, 29, 30l, 32, 34, 35t, 36, 37l, 38.
World Images library: 5, 13r, 17t, 17b, 23t, 23b, 27, 31, 33b, 35b, 37, 39b, 42, 43l, 43r. Every effort has been made to trace the copyright holders, and we apologise in advance for any unintentional omissions. We would be pleased to insert the appropriate acknowledgements in any subsequent edition of this publication.

THE INTERVIEWER

The interviews with Mohamed (the subject of the book) were conducted by Amy De Leal. Amy is a therapist with the International Institute in St. Louis. The International Institute helps refugees and immigrants to independence by teaching English, finding jobs and providing adjustment services to overcome language and cultural barriers.

HOW MOHAMMED WAS CHOSEN

Amy says: *"I chose to ask Mohamed to be involved in this book based on his experiences as a refugee. Due to the circumstances the family endured after the disappearance of Mohamed's father, and the general conditions in Afghanistan at the time they lived there, the family fled to Iran. Mohamed and his family lived as refugees in Iran and Turkey before coming to the United States. They now live in St. Louis, Missouri. As a result of safety concerns and the need to help care for his younger brother and sister, Mohamed does not have many opportunities to socialise with people his own age outside of school. However, he does get to meet teenagers of a variety of nationalities when he visits the International Institute."*

THE INTERVIEW PROCESS

Amy says: *"The interview took place at the International Institute of St. Louis. Mohamed and I sat down and talked during one session that lasted approximately two and a half hours. Mohamed and I both felt that it would be better for him to tell his story in one session. Mohamed said he felt very comfortable relating his experiences as a refugee. He was excited about sharing his story and is proud of what he has been able to achieve despite the difficult circumstances he has had to face."*

Amy De Leal (left) with the subject of the book Mohammed Nazari.

CONTENTS

Introduction

At any one time, about 35 million people worldwide are living in exile from their state of origin – driven out as a result of a natural disaster, or because of a political, military or social situation that has endangered, or threatens to endanger their lives. These people are classed as refugees, asylum seekers or internally displaced persons. Adjusting to a new country and a new culture is not easy. Refugees are affected by this enormous life change in many different ways.

WHAT EXACTLY IS A REFUGEE?

A refugee is a person who is forced to leave their home and seek safety outside of his or her own country. The reason for this might be anything from war, persecution and government oppression, to natural disaster and famine. They might escape on foot to refugee camps outside the borders of their country, or they might travel by boat or aeroplane to the other side of the world.

People flee from these situations because they are seeking safety and protection. In some more privileged countries, governments have set up schemes to help refugees to leave their old country and settle in new countries. There are also many international non-government organisations that assist exiled people. Sometimes, however, people resort to illegal methods of escaping their strife-ridden homelands if they are desperate and there seems no other way out.

THE HISTORY OF REFUGEES

As long as there has been war and famine, there has been a need for human beings to flee their home countries in search of safer territories where they can be assured the basic necessities of life. The word 'refugee' originated in 1573. It was first used to describe the Calvinists who fled to France to escape political repression in the Spanish-controlled Netherlands.

THE RIGHTS OF REFUGEES

Most countries are obliged to offer refugees protection, basic human rights and equal access to public services, in accordance with the Universal Declaration of Human Rights of 1948 and the

Afghanistan is one of a great many countries that have produced refugees due to a political situation.

TOP TEN MAJOR REFUGEE POPULATIONS WORLDWIDE*

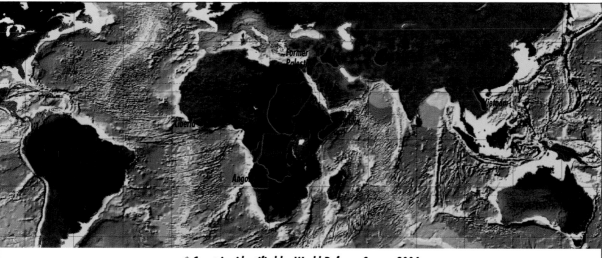

* Countries identified by World Refugee Survey 2004

The burkah is the head-to-toe covering that many Afghan women wear in public.

NUMBER OF PEOPLE CURRENTLY LIVING AS REFUGEES WORLDWIDE*	
Afghan	2,136,000
Sudanese	606,200
Iraqi	600,000
Burundian	531,600
Congolese	530,400
Palestinian	427,900
Somalian	402,200
Vietnamese	363,200
Liberian	353,300
Angolan	329,600

* Statistics from World Refugee Survey 2004

Geneva Convention of 1951. These international laws state that countries are obligated to accept asylum seekers who are in danger of persecution on the basis of race, social group, religion and political affiliation. One of the most basic human rights that should be available to refugees and migrants is the right of non-discrimination. This should entitle refugees to equal opportunities in employment, housing, and government and social benefits without being judged on the basis of their nationality or refugee status. However, this is not always the reality.

Living as a Refugee – *Mohamed's Story*

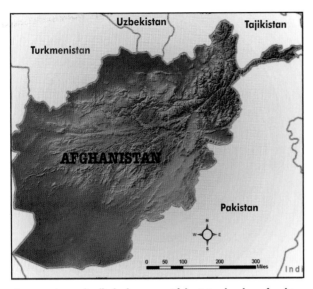

A mountainous, landlocked country, Afghanistan has been fought over for decades.

AFGHANISTAN – A BRIEF HISTORY

The location of Afghanistan at the crossroads of central, western and southern Asia has made it a territory that different empires have invaded and fought over for more than 2,000 years. Fighting has continued almost constantly in Afghanistan over the centuries – the most recent war taking place in 2001, when America invaded following the al-Qaeda attacks on the USA.

Over the centuries, Afghanistan has been controlled by many empires including those of the Persians, the Greeks (led by Alexander the Great), the Arabs, the Turks, the Mongols (led by Genghis Khan) and the British. Finally achieving independence in 1747, Afghanistan's strife did not end there and wars continued throughout the 19th and into the 20th centuries.

In 1973, after 40 years of rule, Afghanistan's King Muhammad Zahir Shah was overthrown by a military coup led by his cousin, Daud Khan. This ended 226 years of monarchy.

Then, in 1978, another coup put a communist government in power. Shortly afterwards, Russia invaded Afghanistan and seized power. The Russian occupation provoked the emergence of a group of Afghan freedom fighters called the 'Mujahidin' who fought against the Soviet army. In 1989, the Russian troops left.

MUJAHIDIN AND THE TALIBAN

In 1992, the Mujahidin declared Afghanistan to be an Islamic state. Mujahidin warlords fought each other in an ongoing civil war until 1996, when a militant Islamic group called the Taliban seized power. The Taliban brought some order to a previously chaotic society. However, they imposed a very extreme system of Islam. Close ties with Pakistan meant that the caves and deserts of the Afghan-Pakistan border areas became a safe haven for terrorists. The Taliban successfully reunited most of Afghanistan, but civil war still continued. Access to food, clean water and employment also decreased during Taliban rule.

AFGHANISTAN FACTS AND FIGURES

- *Population: 28 million*

- *Capital city: Kabul*

- *Geography: Landlocked, mountainous landscape with some plains*

- *Climate: Cold winters and dry, hot summers*

- *Languages: Pashtu (35%); Afghan Persian /Dari (50%); Turkmen and Uzbek (11%)*

- *Religions: Sunni Muslim (84%); Shi'a Muslim (15%)*

The damage sustained to Afghanistan during the US-led War on Terror in 2001–02 affected the whole country and will take many years to repair and rebuild.

SEPTEMBER 11 AND TERRORISM

When America's World Trade Center was attacked and destroyed by two hijacked aeroplanes on September 11, 2001, it was quickly determined that the Islamic terrorist network al-Qaeda, led by Osama bin Laden, was responsible. It was also established that the Taliban were harbouring the Saudi Arabia-born terrorist. When the Taliban refused to hand over bin Laden, America began a military assault.

By January, 2002, the Taliban and al-Qaeda were largely defeated, although most of their leaders and prominent figures (including bin Laden) had gone into hiding. The attacks ended when the Taliban disbanded, however, they resumed guerrilla operations soon after. At this time, there is still a US-led military presence in Afghanistan looking for Osama bin Laden.

RECENT HISTORY TIMELINE

1954–5 Afghanistan is declined military assistance by the USA. The USSR agrees to offer it instead.

1973 Prince Daud organises a coup against the monarchy and proclaims Afghanistan a republic and himself as its first president.

1978 A coup overthrows President Daud. The communist Peoples Democratic Party of Afghanistan (PDPA) assumes power. The people of Afghanistan rebel against the PDPA government shortly afterwards.

1979 4,500 Soviet advisors enter Afghanistan to maintain order. Afghanistan is declared an independent state.

1980 Russia's Red Army engages in a fierce battle with the Mujahidin.

1989 USSR pulls out of Afghanistan.

1991 PDPA government falls.

1993 Mujahidin warlords begin to fight for power.

1996 The Taliban seizes control of 95% of Afghanistan.

2001 (September 11) The US World Trade Center and Pentagon are attacked by hijacked planes.

LATE-2001 US attacks terrorists in retaliation. Hamid Karzai, is sworn in as chairman of a six-month, interim Afghan government.

2004 Afghanistan holds its first democratic elections. Hamid Karzai wins.

CHAPTER ONE: Meet Mohamed

More than three million refugees have returned home to Afghanistan since the fall of the Taliban late in 2001. However, millions of Afghans still remain in exile – many living in poverty, in refugee camps in Pakistan and Iran. Other refugees, like Mohamed Nazari and his family have been more fortunate than many – gaining the right to settle permanently in the United States.

MOHAMED SAYS ...

"My name is Mohamed Nazari and I am 15 years old. I was born in Kabul in Afghanistan. I came to the USA two years ago with my mother, brother and sister. We did not know where our father was at that time. When we left Afghanistan, I was really young – about six or seven years old. First of all our family went to Pakistan, but we only lived there for one month. Then we moved to Tehran, the capital city of Iran, where we lived for two years. After that, we lived in Turkey for two years

Fifteen-year-old Mohamed Nazari is happy to be living in the US after a long journey through many countries.

and then we eventually moved to America. I am the sort of person who likes to know about everything – I like to learn new things and learn all about different places all over the world. I speak four different languages: Iranian, Farsi, Turkish and English. I like to think I have a strong character,

and that I will always be around to help other people when they need me to. I like playing video games and I usually play these games at home with my brother and sister. I like pop music – mainly Iranian stuff like The Black Cats and Sandy. I also like sports and I am especially good at soccer."

Many refugees are forced to live in refugee camps – like these Afghans in Peshawar, Pakistan.

BECOMING A REFUGEE

There are several ways of becoming a refugee. A person can apply from their home country or a country bordering their own, or refugee status can be authorised upon arrival in the new country.

Refugees can be admitted to the US through the 'Overseas Admissions Program'. Staff of US-based non-government organisations and the UN's refugee agency assist US government officers in identifying which refugees are most in need of resettlement.

TEMPORARY HOUSING

Most refugees need to have a contact person, or family, already living in the US before asylum can be granted. These contact people are usually expected to provide temporary housing for the new arrivals until they can find their own accommodation – often with government assistance.

In the UK, refugees are sometimes held in detention centres or housing is organised by the government until their application for asylum has been processed. Those who can are able to live independently in the UK also.

The UK's Migrant Helpline is one of many organisations that offers temporary housing to newly arrived refugees.

"My mother and father are both Muslim and they are both Afghan. They come from different cities to each other. At first, my mother liked somebody else but he went to Germany and never came back. Then she met my father – and they started talking and got together and eventually got married.

My brother Mahdi is 11 and my sister Fereshte is nine years

This is Mohamed's uncle – one of a small number of his extended family still living in Afghanistan.

old. My mother, brother and sister are here with me in America but our father lives in Greece.

When we lived in Afghanistan, my dad worked as an assistant to a truck-driver. He used to deliver fruit and other foods to different cities. One day he went off on a job and didn't come back. We waited and waited, and two years went by and he still didn't come back.

Family mealtimes in the Nazari household are opportunities to eat traditional Afghan foods.

One day my father's friend said to us, 'Maybe he's dead or he's not going to come back and if you guys want, I can take you to Iran. You can sell all your stuff, like your house, and I can take you guys with the money. We didn't want to leave without our father but we were so desperate to leave that we really had no choice.'

Eventually we found out that our father wasn't dead but living in Greece. He doesn't have a house there – he just stays at the park. He always says how cold it is out there and that he cannot sleep on the ground. He tries to find work, but they don't give him any work because he has a kidney problem and the doctor says he cannot work."

REFUGEES – THE CHANGING FIGURE

The US target for resettling refugees was 70,000 a year for most of the 1990s. After September 11, 2001, the US – and much of the Western world – introduced more rigorous security checks on refugee applicants. This slowed entries so much that only 27,000 of the thousands who applied for refugee status were accepted into the US in 2002. Since then, systems have begun to run more smoothly, allowing numbers to creep up annually. A total of 90,000 refugees are expected to settle in the US in 2005.

The United Nations stated that the total number of people seeking asylum has dropped to the lowest level in 17 years. This massive decrease is largely down to the decline in refugees from Iraq and Afghanistan. However, it is also due to the many obstacles placed in the way of refugees by Western states.

REUNITING FAMILIES

During the desperate ordeal of fleeing a troubled country, families are often split up. There are many reasons for this – such as, male family members going to war and losing contact with their families. Whatever the circumstances, it can be hugely traumatic for the families involved.

After the attacks of September 11, 2001, the number of nationalities eligible for the United States' 'family reunification program' for refugee families was reduced from six in 2002 to four in 2003 – due to the number of fraudulent applications. As a result of fraud-prevention measures being introduced, 14 countries will qualify for the scheme from 2005.

Refugees can often be separated from family members for long periods, such as this Afghan family – reunited in Kabul after five years.

"My mother doesn't have any money to send my father. He says there are a lot of Iranian and Afghan people in Greece also looking for work. Sometimes when he calls us we get sad and sometimes I cry because we just want him to come and live with us. My mother started to get sick after our father left and didn't come back. Sometimes when she is sick she sleeps all the time, or sometimes she cries a lot – then she has to go to the hospital for two or three days at a time. Those times are very sad for our family.

It was so hard on the way out of Afghanistan. The Iranian soldiers at the border told us to stop because our car was going too fast. And when the soldiers realised our driver was not going to stop, they shot our tyres out.

We got out of the car and saw there were several guys lying dead on the ground. The guy who was helping us made us hide underground. After two or three hours, he told us to get out and run. We ran for about two hours and my mom got really tired, so I carried her on my back for part of the way, even though I was quite small. At other times, the guy who was with us took her on his back.

After five days and five nights, we finally got to Iran. And the guy who helped us said, 'Now you guys are on your own. I have brought you to Iran and that's all I can do.'

Later, an old woman saw us in the street and said, 'If your

Mohamed can only remember a few details about his journey – because he was just seven years old when he left Afghanistan.

mother can work, I will pay her to clean my house.' Her daughter taught us kids Farsi [the language commonly spoken in Iran today]. After the old lady died, the daughter told us she was going to leave Iran. So we sold everything we owned and used the money to get to Turkey. We took a bus that was supposed to take us to Istanbul. Then the guy that organised it and his friend came onto the bus and called themselves police. But they weren't really police – they just wanted to get money from everyone. But nobody gave them any so they kicked everybody off.

Then an Afghan guy told us there was an organisation called the United Nations and that they would help us go somewhere else. He said everything was expensive in Turkey and that it wasn't a good place for us to be. So he gave us an address and put us on a bus to Ankara [the capital of Turkey]."

Mohamed's bus journey from Iran to Turkey would have taken about 24 hours.

FACTS – TWO DIFFERENT LIVES

In many ways, life in Afghanistan couldn't be more different from life in the USA. Here are some of the major differences:

• Afghanistan is one of the poorest countries in the world. The United States, meanwhile, has one of the world's richest economies.

• Under the Taliban, most freedoms were denied to women in Afghanistan. Even today, Afghan women still experience a lesser social status to men. In the US, however, all people are legally entitled to equal status – regardless of gender, race or religion. However, it is important to note that prejudices still exist in the Western world, despite the legal enforcement of equal rights.

• Afghanistan is a developing country that has endured many years of war. As a result the basic infrastructure (such as electricity, water and sanitation) is either unavailable or unreliable. By contrast, the US is a country where most people have the basic resources they need.

• A total of 39 per cent of Afghan boys are enrolled in school while, until quite recently, girls weren't allowed to attend school at all. In the US, 98 per cent of boys and girls are enrolled in school.

Compared to the privileged Western world, most people in Afghanistan are poor and do not have enough to eat.

13

Mohamed walks to the International Institute with his sister and brother on Saturdays. From here they catch a bus to the mosque.

"There were some people in Ankara who knew how to speak Farsi. They said, 'How did you get here? Do you have passports?' And we said, 'No. We came secretly, without anything.' And, one guy told us that we would have to go to the United Nations office in a different city. There was also a mosque in this city with a small park behind it. We ended up sleeping in that park until the UN could find us somewhere to live. Every week they would say, 'Come back next Friday' until one day, we were sent to this old house where four other mothers with no husbands and about 17 kids lived. One day, this guy told us very quietly, 'Your father's dead – we saw his body.' We said, 'Maybe it was someone else's?' We didn't want to believe it.

After seven or eight months, we were told we had passed which meant we were allowed to stay in Turkey for longer. We were then sent to another *place to live. Here, we tracked down my uncle's phone number in Afghanistan. We called him and he said, 'No your father is not dead – he's alive, but we don't know where he is.'*

After two years, we were told we had to go to Britain. Then, eventually we were told, 'You cannot go to Britain anymore, America wants the Afghans now.' So the UN educated us about how things would be in America and how we should act *when we got there. The first time I went up in an aeroplane was when we flew from Turkey to the US.*

Now I live in the City of St. Louis, in Missouri. It is a good place to live, with friendly people. I have some good friends here. I just think it's a good city because it has a lot of beautiful places; parks and big apartments. It's cool if you see it from the sky."

REFUGEE COMMUNITIES

In the US, some states have particularly high refugee populations. For example, many Afghan refugees have taken up residence in California, Virginia, Texas, Florida, New York, Massachusetts, Arizona, Georgia, Idaho, Washington and Missouri. A local community of Afghan people can often help new refugees to settle more quickly.

Local venues and organised social and cultural events for refugee communities can also assist in the adjustment process. Many NGOs organise such events in their local area.

A CULTURALLY DIVERSE CITY

St. Louis is a city in the American midwest with a population of more than 2.6 million people. St. Louis is a city well known for its cultural diversity (more than 100 different ethnic groups live in the wider area).

The 'Gateway Arch' in St. Louis (completed in 1965), was built to commemorate the westward growth of the US during the 19th century.

Living as a Refugee – *Mohamed's Story*

"There are a lot of kids in our neighbourhood but I don't go out very often, so I don't really know what's going on out there. During the day I'm in school and in the house. I only really go out to do the shopping – and sometimes I take my brother and sister out.

I know some of my neighbours – they are nice people. I don't really think there is anything bad about living in America. We feel safe here.

I go to school where I am in the ninth grade. I can read and write in English, German and Farsi. The school I go to is an international school. There are a lot of teachers and kids from different countries, like Bosnia, America, Pakistan and Hindustan. We talk openly about everybody's different cultures quite a lot. My teachers say I am a good student and I am well-behaved in class.

My favourite subject is science and I also enjoy reading – I have lots of books at home. The teachers are nice to the kids. I didn't go to school in Afghanistan. But I did go for one and a half years in Iran at the first grade, but they took me out because they said, 'You guys don't have passports so you cannot go to school.' So then some Afghans started teaching about 20 kids how to read at home.

My best friends are two Mexican guys, Christian and Victor, and Jafar from Saudi Arabia. We laugh a lot and tell jokes. I don't see them very much because I only have one class with each of them. I don't really hang out with them after school. Last year we had lots of classes together so we were together a lot, but not this year."

Students from over 30 different countries attend Soldan International Studies High School, where Mohamed is a student.

SCHOOLING FOR AFGHANS

In 2002, the United Nations estimated that more then 95 per cent of Afghan children did not go to school. However, since the Taliban were removed from power, that figure has improved dramatically. Over three million children have now returned to school in Afghanistan, including one million girls – many of whom had never before seen the inside of a classroom.

In most democratic societies, all children and young people – including refugees – are entitled to free education. However, due to economic reasons, the Iranian government has recently ruled to charge Afghan children for their schooling. But many Afghan families simply cannot afford this kind of expense (about US$150 per child) and have opted to travel back to the still strife-ridden Afghanistan.

In Afghanistan, crowded classrooms and very little equipment often means two to a desk.

EDUCATION FOR REFUGEES

Many young refugees experience bullying and harassment at school. In countries such as the UK, US and Canada, a number of schools have introduced anti-bullying programmes that include counselling and peer-support for refugees.

School is not always an unhappy place for refugees. A recent survey by Save the Children in the UK found that school was often the highlight of young refugees' lives – particularly if they had come from disruptive backgrounds or had endured traumatic experiences.

Particularly within the last decade, a growing number of secondary schools and independent language schools have designed programmes that address the specific needs of older children with little or no grasp of the English language.

Refugees might experience bullying at school – for their different style of dress, race or cultural habits. Many schools have anti-bullying policies.

CHAPTER TWO: Where is Home?

Many refugees have been unsettled for a long period, often travelling through many countries and dangerous situations, before reaching their final destination. Home can mean lots of places to refugees – some welcoming and others terrifying. No matter how much safer a refugee family might feel when they have settled in the new country, they may still dream of returning home.

The family is important in traditional Afghan culture. Mohamed longs for the day when his father will join the family in America.

Traditional Afghan dress is quite distinctive. Men generally wear loose-fitting long trousers and a shirt while many Afghan women still wear the traditional blue burkah.

MOHAMED SAYS …

"I don't really remember a lot about living in Afghanistan. I only remember that it wasn't very good. I don't remember what the house we lived in looked like, only that it wasn't a good house. It was always very hot there and where we lived was very noisy – people shouting and fighting all the time. Here it is much quieter.

I remember when the Taliban first started taking over. They just forced their way into people's houses and took carpets and things. If people had chickens, cows or lambs, the Taliban took them. They took everything they could carry – and if it was too heavy they would come back for it later. They warned us that before they came back next time, everybody had to leave their houses.

So when we knew they were on their way, most people started running. We ran all the way into the mountains so they couldn't see us."

FACTS – LAWS UNDER THE TALIBAN

During Taliban rule, the people of Afghanistan were subjected to a rigorously enforced system of laws. There were often severe punishments if any of the laws were broken. Under the Taliban:

• TV, music, cinema, singing, dancing and alcohol were all banned.

• Men were forced to wear full, untrimmed beards and baggy trousers.

• Women were prohibited from working and were not allowed out of the house unless accompanied by a male family member.

• Girls were not allowed to attend school.

• Theft was punished by amputating the thief's hand.

• Women caught wearing nail polish would have their fingers cut off.

• Individuals who committed adultery would be stoned to death.

• People were imprisoned for not praying five times a day and at particular times of the day.

• Women who failed to wear the full 'burkah' (loose-fitting garment covering the whole body) would be publicly stoned.

Men who failed to grow long beards during the Taliban years were beaten in punishment.

"But my grandmother and grandfather couldn't walk very far because they were quite old, so they made us leave without them. They said, 'We don't care what happens to us. You guys just go.' So we did, we left, and when we came back we saw that the Taliban had cut my grandmother and grandfather's heads off.

The Taliban also sometimes set everything on fire, or they had parties and ate all the food and then just trashed the place and left.

The Taliban killed so many people. When we were living in Turkey, these guys brought round some videos that showed what was going on in Afghanistan. These people back in Afghanistan would send the videos to lots of different places

One of the many things banned by the Taliban were films. This group of Taliban officials burnt hundreds of reels of film in front of downtown Kabul's Zaynab cinema.

where Afghans lived so that people like us could see what was going on in our country. We watched so many people dying – the videos showed how the people died.

I remember in Afghanistan, all the streets smelt bad. The Taliban would just kill people and the blood would run like rivers of water. They would take a person and slash their throat and then they would just take another one and do it again.

The Taliban ordered women to stay in the house and do the housework. If they saw a woman outside, they would take her to the soccer stadium (although no-one was allowed to play soccer there) – then they would shoot her there."

WHO ARE THE TALIBAN?

The Taliban is an Islamist movement that ruled most of Afghanistan from 1996 until 2001. Only three countries (the United Arab Emirates, Pakistan, and Saudi Arabia) ever officially acknowledged the Taliban as a legitimate government. The Taliban emerged after ongoing rebel wars, and, while they created some stability in Afghanistan after two decades of war and anarchy, their fundamentalist Islamic laws attracted mass criticism. Several years after their defeat in 2001, the Taliban is now a militia operating in parts of Afghanistan that are outside the control of the government.

OSAMA BIN LADEN & AL-QAEDA

Al-Qaeda is an international terrorist network. Its mission is to rid Muslim countries of the influence of the West – replacing governments with fundamentalist Islamic regimes. Osama bin Laden is the leader of al-Qaeda and allegedly the man behind the attacks that destroyed America's World Trade Center and damaged part of the Pentagon. Bin Laden is still on the run from US forces who continue to hunt for him in Afghanistan and Pakistan.

When it was in power, the Taliban gave al-Qaeda support and security. Today, there are al-Qaeda bases all over the world, although after the September 11 attacks, many members have been apprehended by police.

Osama bin Laden, leader of al-Qaeda, is probably the world's most wanted man after he allegedly admitted responsibility for the September 11 attacks.

"*And they would make everyone go to the mosque five times a day. Then, even if you went fives times, they would still say, 'Go back!' And we would say, 'We already went five times.' But they would just say, 'What did I say?' And if you said that you wouldn't go, they would just kill you.*

Everybody was scared of the Taliban. There was nothing to be happy about when they were in power. You never knew if they were going to come to your house or if they would approach you in the street.

I do miss Afghanistan. I just want to go and see it again. I don't know when that will be. I miss the old houses and friends – mainly the people. But who knows how many of those people are still alive or where they are now.

One of the hardest things about being a refugee is leaving loved ones behind in difficult situations and not knowing whether they are alive or dead.

Day after day we were scared about what was going to happen next when we lived in Afghanistan. One day, one of my friends was playing with this bomb that had fallen down in our neighbourhood. He said he didn't think anything was going to happen to him and he just threw it up in the air and it came back down and 'BOOM' – it killed him."

More than six years of drought have contributed to severe food and water shortages across Afghanistan.

FAMINE AND POVERTY

As a result of many problems affecting the country including years of continuous warfare, a harsh, unforgiving climate and lack of arable land – Afghanistan has been one of the world's poorest, most underdeveloped countries for many years. Following a lengthy period of civil war, droughts and poor harvests, Afghanistan has endured many years of famine. When the US invaded Afghanistan in 2001, the country was suffering the worst drought in 30 years.

Today, seven million people are vulnerable to famine, and healthcare facilities are not sufficient to deal with the number of malnourished people or those suffering from diseases, such as: pneumonia, tuberculosis, diarrhoea, malaria and measles.

CHILD SOLDIERS

Many young boys fought against the Soviet invasion of Afghanistan in 1979, and boys were recruited to train as soldiers throughout the remainder of the 20th century. When the Taliban was in power (1996–2001), there were many reports that boys as young as ten years old were forced to fight. Similarly, the Northern Alliance (who fought against the Taliban) were proven to be using children as young as 11, despite publicly declaring that their soldiers had to be 18 to join.

The reality for many boys and young men in Afghanistan during the time the Taliban was recruitment into the army.

"I think we were lucky to get refugee status in America. One day felt like one year in Afghanistan. Nobody was happy there – not happy like we are here. When we left Afghanistan, it was still a long time before we felt safe. We were afraid sometimes when we were in Iran because people kept telling us to leave their country and go home.

When we were in Iran, a lot of the Afghan kids would run wild and fight with each other. They would do things like take some food an old woman was selling and throw it in the street. They would just pick on people like her to prove something – because they would get in serious trouble for fighting with the Iranian boys. I guess they just wanted to show the Iranian guys they could fight.

We were very poor when we lived in Afghanistan – everybody was. There was not a lot of food for the people and not many stores even if you did have money to buy things you needed. Some people looked for vegetables in the mountains and took them home to eat. So life in America is much easier.

American people have been welcoming since we got here and no-one in my family has really found it difficult to adjust to life here.

Before, I wanted to go to school but I didn't go to school in Afghanistan. Then, I only went for one and a half years in Iran and one month in Turkey. Now, I get to go full-time.

When we first got here and we didn't know any English, it was hard getting to know other kids at school.

Mohamed finds life much quieter and safer in the US, although he is aware there are still dangers on the streets. This is one reason why he doesn't go out much.

Mohamed is a true friend and role model to his siblings. As well as walking to the bus stop with them, he also cooks for them when his mother is not well.

But after we learned English, we could understand what the other kids were saying and then we could talk back to them. Basically, if you can't speak English, people aren't going to want to bother with you, are they? But once we could communicate with each other, it was no problem.

Everybody's friendly here – they just say, 'Where you from?' – they don't care what country you come from. Most of the people in St. Louis are American but that doesn't really affect me because I don't spend much time with other people anyway.

The school I go to is a bit different to some schools because it is an international school. Like, my friends are from Mexico and Saudi Arabia and other places."

FACTS – EXPECTATIONS VS REALITY

For refugees, expectations of their new home country can be romantic and unrealistic. These inaccurate expectations can have a big impact on how they settle into their new life.

• Many refugees expect free healthcare, such as there is in certain parts of the world. In the UK, for example, healthcare is free to all residents. However, in the US, a person must have medical insurance in order to see a doctor or dentist.

• Some refugees expect to qualify for disability benefits when they reach the US because they have high blood pressure, or consider themselves 'too old' to work. Under US law, however, they often do not qualify.

• A number of refugees expect to be much better off financially when they reach the new country. Many expect a big house and enough money to buy everything they need. The reality is more often: several family members sharing a bedroom, parents struggling to find work and not having enough money to send children on to higher education.

Mohamed and his family share the same bedroom. His mother and sister sleep on one side of the room while the boys sleep on the other.

CHAPTER THREE: Adjusting to a New Life

Moving to a new country as a refugee can be a life-changing experience in many ways. The advantages – safety, security, food, freedom – are immediately felt. However, individuals might also experience acute anxiety about the plight of their country and those they have left behind, as well as culture shock when faced with a completely different and alien way of life. The host country should be prepared to offer newcomers all the support they need to adjust.

Mohamed and Mahdi enjoy playing video games in their spare time – a hobby he would never have even imagined back in Afghanistan.

MOHAMED SAYS:

"I don't really talk to anyone about how I feel about things. My friends are often busy and want to go and play outside (which I don't really do very often). Also, my mom won't let me hang out with the other Afghan kids in St. Louis. She thinks they just make trouble and are a bad influence on me.

Every day at school, these kids get suspended for five days or something – and when they come back to school they keep doing the same stuff and getting into the same kind of trouble. They often just skip school. And when the police ask them, 'Why are you guys not in school?' these kids just tell the policemen that they have dropped out."

Like many refugees who have endured trauma in their home country and the upheaval of moving to a new country, Mohamed's mother suffers from depression.

PSYCHOLOGICAL IMPACT

Afghans are very private people and emotional issues are not generally discussed. Therefore, many people with mental-health problems due to traumatic experiences or things they have witnessed find it difficult to engage in the kind of 'talk therapy' common in the West.

The World Health Organization estimates that 95 per cent of Afghans have been psychologically affected in some way by decades of war and violence in Afghanistan. Despite these staggering figures, however, there are only four mental hospitals in the country. This is a growing concern as millions of refugees are now returning to their homeland.

CULTURE SHOCK

Refugees can also experience culture shock upon arriving in their new country. If they have come from a deprived country where poverty is the norm and food is scarce, the consumerism and fast-food culture of the West must be a big surprise. Also, when a family speak minimal English, knowing how to communicate their needs, and even such simple things as doing the grocery shopping must seem like major obstacles.

Even something as basic as grocery shopping can be a major hurdle for people with no local language ability or knowledge of products and the way things are done.

"I didn't know much about the US before we moved here. When we arrived we were very happy. It was coming into winter and it started to snow soon after we arrived. That was exciting for my brother and sister because it was the first time they had seen snow. In Turkey and Iran it got very cold but there was only ever rain, no snow.

When we grow up, our mom wants us to be doctors or something. She wants to go back to Afghanistan with my father one day and she hopes we will be able to buy them a house. She says she tries hard to give us what we need and that we should do the same for them when we are grown up. My mother won't learn to drive here or learn English because she is just waiting to go back to Afghanistan. When that happens, I will stay living in the US but will go back to Afghanistan to visit my parents.

I don't feel like I have to marry an Afghan woman. My mother doesn't care who I end up with – I don't even feel that they have to be a Muslim. It would only be important that we belonged to the same faith as each other. If she was Christian, I would become Christian too, or I would want her to change to be Muslim.

I don't really have an opinion about arranged marriages. I guess I would be fine with it if she was a good lady – but if she was not a nice person, I wouldn't be happy about it.

Afghan women are so much happier now they are free. Now they can go shopping, and go to work

Young refugees often find it easier to settle into their new culture than their parents, generally picking up the new language much faster.

or they can go to the park with their children or husbands. Before, under the Taliban, they just had to stay in the house – they couldn't even go to the mosque. Under the Taliban, women in Afghanistan were like birds in cages. I think it is good that men and women in America are equal."

Western influences in Afghanistan – such as football – were forbidden under the Taliban.

ADOPTING A NEW CULTURE

Many cultural practices in the West must seem completely alien to refugees who have never encountered the Internet, the latest technology or Western television programmes. This is particularly the case for cultures that have been sheltered from the influences of other countries – as Afghanistan was. Fashions and dating may also be a completely new experience for teenage refugees. In traditional Afghan culture, for example, single girls are not allowed to socialise without their families being present. Yet in the West, it is generally quite acceptable for young women to socialise independently.

Young refugees might be tempted to join their peers who are dating and going to parties – and yet there may still be pressures from their families for young men to marry a 'pure' woman who has been sheltered from the outside world.

ARRANGED MARRIAGES

Traditionally, young Afghans are told from an early age that their spouse will be chosen for them. It is very important for all family members to uphold the family 'honour' at all times, so to deny an arranged marriage is seen likely to result in the family disowning the child. Statistics show that the divorce rate for arranged marriages is much lower than marrying for love. However, research also shows that the pressure a married couple encounters from both society as a whole, and from the respective families, suggests that divorce is often not an option.

Traditional Afghan weddings are occasions when ritual, ceremony and family honour reign supreme.

"My friends and I ask each other lots of questions about our different cultures. They say, 'What are the presents like there?', 'What food do you eat there?', 'What are the people like there?' and 'What are the soldiers like?' – things like that. And you tell them how it is and they tell you how it is in their country. We just ask each other when we want to learn – friends just want to know about each other and where they have come from. As soon as we got better at English, we all started making lots of friends. I don't really mix with a lot of Afghan guys here. Mainly because my Mom doesn't let me. I haven't really found it difficult to adjust to life in America. But because we are still learning English though, sometimes school can be hard. Sometimes in Social Studies, I get Cs, Ds or even Fs. Sometimes I have so much homework, I don't know which project to do first! I also have to help my sister and brother with their homework. I'd like to get a part-time job soon, maybe, like, at Blockbuster, or somewhere else like that. I had a job last summer washing dishes at the bakery store. Every summer the International Institute finds teenagers jobs if they want them.

Mohamed is a dedicated student, although he finds it difficult sometimes to get good grades, because English is not his first language.

When I first arrived here I was 13 and they told me I was too young to get a summer job.

When I finish school I would like to be a doctor. I like helping people. It is so much harder to find a job in Afghanistan. In Afghanistan, no-one would tell me I could be anything I wanted to be when I grew up. But in America, people tell you to follow your dreams and that you can take up any career you want.

I don't really stay that informed about what is happening in Afghanistan although sometimes I watch the News on TV. When I hear that things are difficult there it makes me sad. We wish other Afghans could get out of there like we have – that they could be free like us."

On top of his own ever-increasing level of homework, Mohamed helps his younger siblings with theirs.

FACTS – PREJUDICE AND DISCRIMINATION

Refugees often encounter prejudice when settling in a new country. This can be on the grounds of race or ethnic origin, religion or refugee status, and it can manifest in many different ways.

• Refugees, like many minority groups, can experience discrimination in many areas of public life, such as: in the workplace and when seeking accommodation, and from public services and facilities. It can involve harassment, vilification and sometimes actual violence.

• Some sections of the media and even certain politicians have described asylum seekers and refugees as 'invaders' and 'illegal immigrants'.

• After the September 11 attacks, there were many cases reported in the US of Arab-American organisations, Islamic centres and mosques being bombed or burnt down by anti-Muslim activists.

• In 2004, the French government passed a controversial law that banned the wearing of religious clothing and symbols by school students. Some believe this law will encourage ethnic minorities to integrate more into French society. Others believe it violates the right to freedom of religious expression.

A recent law in France has been criticised for compromising freedom of religious expression.

CHAPTER FOUR: Afghan or American?

Once the initial hurdles of settling into a new country are overcome, there are still many things to adapt to. Although it might seem strange at first, many refugees will come to accept and even appreciate belonging to two cultures. Some will want to blend in with the crowd, keeping their religion and heritage private, while others will prefer to maintain their traditional ways of doing certain things.

MOHAMED SAYS ...

"My family are Shi'ite Muslim. I think we come from the Tajik tribe but I am not sure. The traditional Afghan festivals my family celebrates are Nau-Roz [the first day of the Afghan solar calendar] and Eid which comes after Ramadan. Although my family are Muslim, we are not orthodox. We practise our religion by copying what our mother does. We go to mosque to pray on Saturdays. They don't have an Afghan mosque in our neighbourhood. There's a Pakistani one, but they are mad. We tried to go there but they changed the locks twice so we couldn't get in. But it beats being in Afghanistan because there we would have to put up with killing and fighting."

ISLAMIC CENTER / MASJID
3843 WEST PINE
ISLAMIC FOUNDATION
EST. 1974

Mohamed's family take the bus to mosque after problems at the Pakistani one in their neighbourhood.

THE RELIGIONS OF AFGHANISTAN

While Islam is by far the most dominant religion in Afghanistan (99 per cent of the population), other religions exist alongside it, such as Christianity, Hinduism, Judaism, Buddhism and Bahai. The religion of Islam was founded by the Prophet Mohammad in the 7th century and today has 935 million followers worldwide.

A person who belongs to the Islamic faith is called a Muslim. Islam split into two groups – Sunni (about 85 per cent of the world's Muslim population) and Shi'a or Shi'ite (about 15 per cent). Muslims worship at a temple, called a 'mosque'. They believe there is one true god called Allah and they study his 'eternal word' – a book of rules for life called the Qur'an. Orthodox muslims are obliged to practise regular acts of worship, including praying five times a day.

Muslims attend regular prayer sessions at their local Islamic temple known as a mosque, such as this one above.

MUSLIM FESTIVALS

ASHURA: The most important period for Shi'ite Muslims which occurs during the first 10 days of the New Year.

RAMADAN: The ninth month of the Muslim calendar when Muslims fast during the day and visit family in the evenings.

EID UL-FITR: A three-day feast that occurs after the fasting month of Ramadan.

EID UL-ADHA: A three-day feast that concludes with an annual pilgrimage to Mecca in Saudi Arabia.

Thousands of Muslims flock to Mecca during Eid Ul-Adha to visit the holiest Muslim shrine, the Ka'aba.

"The people in America have been kind and helpful to us since we arrived. We have nothing to worry about here. They help us by giving us food stamps and things. Both my mother and my sister are on disability benefits, so we get money from social services for that.

I don't know much about my Afghan culture because I was so young when we left there. But I am proud to be Afghan. Sometimes we eat traditional meals at home. When my mom is feeling OK she tells us to go play and she does all the cooking and housework. But when she is sick, she spends a lot of time sleeping – at those times I will cook for my brother and sister – things like potato chips, eggs and chicken.

I don't really feel like I've changed much since I moved to the US. I was a quiet sort of person there as well. I also stayed home a lot there, too. Back there it was because there was so much fighting in the streets and so I have learned never to go

Even though he acknowledges that America is now his home country, Mohamed will always call himself Afghan.

out of the house (unless I have to). I try to go out more now I am here, but just find I can't sometimes. I still think of myself as Afghan even though I am in America. When I am with Afghan people,

I speak in the old language and do the kinds of things I used to do when I lived in Afghanistan. And when I am with white people, I kind of do the same things that they do."

Mohamed's mother usually cooks traditional Afghan meals for the family.

MAINTAINING A DUAL IDENTITY

For some refugees, it can be a struggle to balance their original culture and the way of life in the new country – yet for many this 'dual identity' is something to be proud of. Many Afghan refugees living in the US call themselves 'Afghan-Americans' and in some parts of America there are Afghan communities – areas where a number of Afghan families have settled together. In these environments, Afghan culture is celebrated and allowed to flourish. Many Afghan families maintain certain traditions within the home environment, such as in their style of cooking, the types of music they listen to and the festivals they celebrate.

STIGMA OF TERRORISM

Before September 11, 2001, most people knew little about Afghanistan. But because of the huge influence of the media, many have now come to associate Afghanistan solely with terrorism. This has impacted on how many Afghan-Americans were treated post-9/11 – many Islamic organisations and Arabian or Asian people were attacked or told to go home, even if they were born in the US and weren't actually Afghan.

Terrorists are political and/or religious activists who use violent methods to achieve what they want.

"I don't think people treat me differently because I'm Afghan. There are plenty of other guys at my school who are Afghan, so it doesn't seem that different. My friends and I don't really talk about our different cultures that much. I feel like this is my home now – as much as I did in Afghanistan. I have other friends who are also refugees and they've got their own stories to tell. But most of the time, my friends and I just want to play. Or we like to tell jokes and laugh about things.

I like the fact there are a lot of cultures living side-by-side – most people are quite similar really.

I don't care what nationality a person is. I like everybody – I don't mind where they come from.

A typical day for me goes something like this: I take the bus to school with my brother and sister. When I get there, I spend my day inside the classrooms, then, after that – I come back home and do homework – that's about all I do. I spend lunchtimes with the guys – my friends. We sit together at a big table where we talk and eat and say things to each other, like, 'What have you been doing?', and when another guy has had the same class after you, he might say, 'What did you study

Mohamed and his brother Mahdi catch a bus to the mosque on Saturdays where they study the Qur'an.

The Nazari family are happy living in St. Louis. Mohamed describes his neighbours as friendly and the suburban streets very quiet.

in class?' If it's an easy thing, they go to class — and if not, sometimes they skip.

I seem to spend most of my time at school. And then, when I get home I usually have a lot of homework to do. I also help my brother and sister with their homework, although lately they have started going to after-school programmes and tutoring at Kingdom House.

At home, I also help my mom with the chores, like clearing up and cooking dinner sometimes, too.

Sometimes I like to be alone, but other times I want to be with other kids when we can all talk to each other about what's been going on in our lives. It makes me happy that I have plenty of freedom to see friends and go places if I want to these days. I also like reading, too — we have a lot of books in the house."

FACTS – EMPLOYMENT FOR AFGHANS

Even for the most skilled Afghans, it is difficult to establish whether the struggle to find work is greater in their home country or in their country of asylum.

• Recently, the City University of London conducted a survey and found that only 29 per cent of refugees living in the UK were employed.

• Inability to speak the language and lack of local work experience can put refugees at a disadvantage when job-seeking.

• Many refugees find their professional skills aren't recognised in the new country. Refugees trained as doctors, nurses and teachers can find themselves working as labourers or shop assistants – if they can source work at all.

• The unemployment rate in Afghanistan is 78 per cent; while in the US, the official rate is 5.4 per cent.

• Afghanistan's economy is greatly dependent on the growth and sale of opium plants which are used to make the drug heroin.

The plants that produce the drug heroin grow very easily in Afghanistan's hot, dry climate.

CHAPTER FIVE: Looking to the Future

Multiple losses of people, places and possessions, combined with the culture shock of life in a new country, can be a lot for a young person to adjust to. However, evidence suggests that most young refugees adapt incredibly quickly to their new way-of-life, with the majority feeling determined to be successful in their chosen career and generally feeling optimistic about the future.

MOHAMED SAYS ... *"I don't really think about what I'll do when I grow up. I know I want to be a doctor and work in a hospital, although at the moment I also want to be a movie star.*

I would like to live in California one day. I haven't been there yet but I have heard it's a good place as some friends of our family live there. They tell us the climate is good and that a lot of Afghans live in their neighbourhood – they say it's a really good place to live.

Right now what I really wish is that Afghanistan was the same as the US is – where everybody is free. There is nothing bad about living in the US. It is getting to be much more free in Afghanistan than it ever used to be though.

Before, the Taliban forced men to have long beards and things like that – but now

Mohamed hopes to travel to Germany one day – where a lot of his family now lives.

that they don't have to, most men have shaved their beards off. If I were president of Afghanistan or America, I would make sure everybody in the world was free."

Mohamed has made an admirable effort to settle into his new life in the US. One day he hopes to visit Afghanistan again. But for now, he has found a place where he feels safe, free and happy.

This English class is one of the many services offered to refugees by agencies like the International Institute.

LEARNING THE LANGUAGE

The most important skill that most refugees need when they arrive in their new country is knowledge of the local language. Asylum seekers and refugees settling in the UK who wish to learn English can do so for a minimal fee, while some courses, run by non-profit organisations, are free. There are also organisations that provide childcare and money to cover transport costs.

In the US, refugees can learn English through community-education classes for an affordable fee. Some non-government organisations offer special 'youth programmes' for young refugees. These programmes include after-school language classes and homework assistance, as well as opportunities for socialising, cultural events and help in building self-esteem.

WORK AND TRAINING SCHEMES

Some asylum countries offer basic skills-training courses to help refugees towards finding employment. Many of these schemes include work-placement opportunities and mentoring schemes. Young refugees often feel pressure to find employment, so that they can contribute to family finances or help other family members to migrate from the strife-ridden country. Unfortunately, refugees find there are few employment opportunities for them in most countries today.

Basic job-training courses provide refugees with skills necessary for finding employment.

LIFE AFTER WAR

After 20 years of war and destruction, Afghanistan is slowly being rebuilt. Since the War on Terror ended the Taliban rule in 2001, the quality of life has improved for the Afghan people. But there is still a very long way to go. The Afghan people are no longer ruled by the fundamentalist Islamic regime that was imposed by the Taliban. Children are now free to go to school, women are allowed to stop wearing the burkah if they choose to (although many still opt to wear it) and to leave the house unaccompanied by men (although many are still harassed when they do). Despite these, and many other liberating steps forward, the war has left much of Afghanistan in ruins which is going to take many years to rebuild.

Food is still scarce due to droughts, poor economy and the after-effects of war. People are working hard at rebuilding their towns and cities – and their own lives – but even so, most people have to live on US$1 a day.

During the Taliban rule in Afghanistan, no girls were able to attend school and only a small percentage of boys.

A NEW GOVERNMENT

At the end of 2004, Hamid Karzai became Afghanistan's first elected president. The US-backed president has promised his people that his government will bring peace to the war-torn nation and an end to the economy's dependence on the drug trade. Afghanistan is currently by far the world's leading producer of opium (the drug used to make heroin). According to the United Nations, the opium trade accounts for more than 60 per cent of Afghanistan's economy.

Afghanistan's new constitution has been praised by the USA as the most progressive in the region. The UN and the USA have promised to stand by Afghanistan, helping the new government to restore peace and security to the country. The total cost of rebuilding Afghanistan is hard to calculate but is bound to run into billions of dollars.

Hamid Karzai became interim president in Afghanistan in 2002, after the US-led military assault was over. At the end of 2004, he was re-elected by the Afghan people.

ENCOURAGED TO RETURN

Now that peace and quality of life are improving in Afghanistan, the International Organisation for Migration is encouraging Afghan refugees with professional skills to return to help rebuild the country. Afghans who go home by choice generally qualify for the grants under the 'voluntary assisted returns' package. Since the fall of the Taliban, over three million Afghan refugees have repatriated.

TERRORISM AND 9/11

The majority of Afghan-Americans condemned the al-Qaeda attacks on America, and all subsequent acts of terrorism committed in the name of Islam around the world. Afghan-American people are able to understand, perhaps more than most of the rest of the Western world, what it is like to suffer at the hands of terrorists.

Despite this, however, opinions are divided among American Muslims (as they are across the world, amongst all races, cultures and religions) about whether military action in Afghanistan after 9/11 was morally justified. Many people are dubious as to the motives of President George W Bush and his administration.

MILITARY PRESENCE

Even though the US-led War on Terror has ended, the United States continues to have a military presence in Afghanistan. The US government maintains that its troops must remain in Afghanistan as long as the Taliban and militant warlords remain a threat to peace. As is the case with attitudes to the war itself, there are many conflicting perspectives on whether the continuing US presence in Afghanistan is a good thing. Some have raised the concern that Afghanistan might never stand alone unless it is given the opportunity to do so.

FACTS – AFGHANISTAN'S ONGOING NEEDS

The effort, time and cost involved in rebuilding Afghanistan after 20 years of war are expected to be massive. Priorities include:

• Establishing effective security systems, including police and justice systems, maintaining the presence of peace-keeping forces until the country is safe enough for them to withdraw.

• Clearing away the thousands of mines scattered across the country and seizing illegally owned guns from citizens.

• Rebuilding roads, buildings, hospitals and houses; sowing crops and building water-treatment plants and irrigation systems.

• Implementing new national systems such as schooling and healthcare, and restoring the media and other vital communication systems.

• Helping people to start up companies and businesses that will increase the number of job opportunities for local people.

Muslims worldwide, including those living in the US at the time, were horrified by the terrorist attacks on America's World Trade Center and Pentagon in 2001.

41

CHAPTER SIX: Support Networks

Millions of refugees are currently living in exile all over the world. Some are forced to flee with no assistance, sometimes they have to walk for days or spend everything they have on a tenuous escape plan that might not necessarily succeed. Government-funded organisations and hundreds more non-government aid organisations work hard to assist desperate refugees to reach a safer environment and to integrate with local communities.

The UNHCR is the official international organisation responsible for overseeing all issues relating to immigration and refugees.

THE OFFICE OF THE UNITED NATIONS HIGH COMMISSIONER FOR REFUGEES

The Office of the United Nations High Commissioner for Refugees (UNHCR) was founded in 1950, by the United Nations General Assembly. The UNHCR is responsible for leading an international operation that endeavours to protect refugees and resolve refugee problems worldwide. The organisation also assists internally displaced persons, asylum seekers and returnees (refugees who have returned to their own countries). The UNHCR is funded through annual donations and the governments of the USA and Japan are the major donors.

THE GENEVA CONVENTION

The 1951 Geneva Convention relating to the Status of Refugees, along with its 1967 Protocol, is the main law outlining the rights of refugees. Where the original Convention only concerned persons who had become refugees as a result of events occurring prior to 1 January, 1951, the Protocol extended the boundaries to relate to citizens of all countries. A total of 142 countries signed the Geneva Convention and a further 141 signed the Protocol. Countries that have not signed either are mainly in Asia and the Middle East.

In Europe, in addition to the Refugee Convention, the right to asylum is guaranteed by the EU's Charter of Fundamental Rights. There have also been many official commissions and reports conducted all over the world into the changing needs and circumstances of refugees.

INTERNATIONAL ORGANISATIONS

Many government-run organisations that work towards assisting refugees have a global influence. Examples of these International Organisations (IOs) include the United Nations International Children's Fund (UNICEF), UNHCR, Economic and Social Council, World Food Program (WFP), Food and Agriculture Organization (FAO), and the International Committee of the Red Cross.

In most asylum countries there are many government services and NGOs that have been set up to help refugees.

Many organisations have representatives in countries where people are suffering. In Afghanistan, dozens of agencies are trying to get food to people facing the threat of famine.

NON-GOVERNMENT ORGANISATIONS

A Non-government Organisation (or NGO) is a non-profit-making organisation of individuals motivated by humanitarian and/or religious values. These groups play a major role in providing urgently needed relief to victims of civil and military conflicts, and natural disasters. Most NGOs employ volunteers who work 'on the ground' – often providing faster and more effective results than government bodies.

THE US RESETTLEMENT PROGRAM

In the US, the government's 'resettlement program' is a huge operation with many departments, including:

• The Immigration and Naturalization Service (INS) which determines who meets the requirements to become refugees.

• The Department of State (DOS) which arranges flights for refugees and gives funding to the NGOs who help refugees to settle in when they first arrive.

• The Department of Health and Human Services (HHS) which supplies cash and medical assistance to arriving refugees.

43

A recent UK study has shown that refugee children are three times more likely to have psychological problems than non-refugee children. This highlights the need for refugee children to receive counselling and support upon arrival.

THE BUSINESS OF HELPING PEOPLE

Dozens of non-government aid organisations worldwide play a significant role in assisting the UNHCR in its efforts to help refugees. Other organisations like the International Institute of St. Louis, Refugees International, the United States Committee for Refugees, the Red Cross, CARE, UNICEF, Médecins Sans Frontières and the International Rescue Committee work hard to help people in extreme situations flee to safer places.

The media also plays a big part in keeping the world informed of the plight of refugees all over the world. Media also provides a useful forum for organisations appealing for public donations.

REFUGEES WORLDWIDE

Refugees are often forced to flee because of war or a corrupt government. In these situations, people are often killed mercilessly, children kidnapped, women raped, and houses and schools destroyed. Governments may also restrict services (such as healthcare) and food from needy people.

Natural disaster, famine and epidemics are other reasons for large numbers of people to leave their country.

REFUGEE CAMPS

Some refugees manage to reach temporary accommodation in camps situated in

Refugees often find that the threats present at refugee camps are not dissimilar to those from which they have fled.

neighbouring countries. However, these camps are not necessarily the safe havens they should be. They are often unequipped for dealing with the numbers and needs of these desperate, often traumatised people. Often there is not enough food or healthcare available.

Women and children make up the majority of refugees and displaced persons worldwide. This is because women are often forced to flee alone or with their children because their husbands have either been killed, are in jail, are fighting, or have already fled or gone into hiding. This can make women very vulnerable to violence and sexual assault throughout their journey and, especially, in refugee camps.

RETURNING HOME

For most refugees, the ultimate resolution to their plight and what they most desire would be to eventually return home without fear. Unfortunately, a country that has endured devastating catastrophes can take many years to be rebuilt and returned to a peaceful, prosperous place to live, even with the financial assistance of other countries. Refugees returning to war-ravaged countries such as Afghanistan and Iraq face a long road to recovery as they rebuild their lives and their homes.

HOW YOU CAN HELP

1. BE INFORMED OF THE ISSUES
Which countries are producing refugees and why? Watch the television news, read newspapers, visit the websites of official government and non-government organisations; most are regularly updated.

2. WRITE A LETTER
You could write or email the UN Secretary-General, or your local MP, urging them to take more action to intervene on behalf of refugees.

3. MAKE A DONATION
You can donate as much or as little as you like to any official charity or aid organisation. Make sure it is a registered charity. Details of how to make a donation will be listed on all individual organisation's websites.

4. SIGN AN ONLINE PETITION
There are many petitions on the Internet you can sign protesting against asylum seekers being jailed unreasonably, the conditions of refugee camps, and so on. (Make sure the petition is on an official charity's website.)

5. ARRANGE FOR AN ORGANISATION TO COME AND TALK AT YOUR SCHOOL
Generating greater awareness of the problems can really help.

6. VOLUNTEER WORK
Many organisations are grateful for volunteer workers in all sorts of areas. Check websites for details.

7. ORGANISE A FUNDRAISER
Engage the help of an adult and arrange for an event, clearly stating why you are raising money and for who. Some organisations might supply you with flyers and official collector's badges etc.

GLOSSARY

AL-QAEDA International terrorist organisation that calls for the use of violence in bringing about an end to non-Islamic governments.

ASYLUM Protection granted by a country to someone who has been forced to become a refugee.

ASYLUM SEEKER Refugee who has applied for asylum but is waiting for his or her case to be decided.

BURKAH Loose garment worn by Afghan women in public that covers the entire body and face.

COUP A sudden seizure of power from a government.

CULTURE SHOCK Feeling of confusion and isolation when subjected to a new way-of-life.

DISCRIMINATION Judging something unfairly based on prior beliefs.

DUAL IDENTITY Drawing from, or identifying with, two different cultures.

ETHNIC Relating to religion, race, culture or nationality.

EXILE Being forced to live away from one's own country.

FAMINE Drastic shortage of food affecting a wide area.

IMMIGRANT Person who leaves one country to settle in another.

INFRASTRUCTURE Basic services necessary to the functioning and well-being of a society.

INTERNALLY DISPLACED PERSONS People who have been driven from their homes due to conflict or persecution but who remain within the borders of their country.

ISLAM International religion that worships a single God, called Allah. Followers believe that Mohamed was the last prophet on Earth.

MENTORING SCHEMES Programmes that assist people by teaching them new skills that will help them get by in society.

MILITANT Aggressive person or organisation.

MOSQUE Muslim temple of worship.

MUJAHIDIN A force of Muslim military fighters.

MUSLIM A person who belongs to the Islamic religious faith.

NORTHERN ALLIANCE A political group in Afghanistan who practised a liberal form of Islam and who opposed the Taliban.

OPPRESSION Harsh, cruel and controlling rule.

ORTHODOX Traditional and conservative religion.

PERSECUTION Punishment or harassment because of race, ethnic group, gender or politics.

PREJUDICE Dislike or negative opinion formed without any actual experience or knowledge of the individual person or facts.

QUR'AN Sacred text of Islam, believed by Muslims to contain the words of God as revealed to the prophet Mohamed.

REFUGEE Person who has been forced to leave his or her country.

SANCTUARY Safe place.

SHI'ITE (SHI'A) A branch of Islam with many followers in Afghanistan.

STIGMA A negative association or prejudice attached to something.

SUNNI The branch of Islam that accepts the first four Islamic leaders as Mohamed's rightful successors.

TALIBAN The militant Islamic group that took over government of Afghanistan in 1996 and remained in power until 2001.

TERRORISM Unlawful use of force or violence from an organised group whose intent is to intimidate or influence governments.

UNITED NATIONS International organisation founded in 1945 to promote and uphold international security and peace between nations.

VILIFICATION To make vicious or abusive statements about someone or something.

FURTHER INFORMATION

AMNESTY INTERNATIONAL
The world's largest international organisation that actively campaigns for human rights. www.amnesty.org

EUROPEAN COUNCIL ON REFUGEES & EXILES (ECRE)
A European network of NGOs that assists refugees. ECRE aims to strengthen the capacity of, and co-operation between, NGOs and other organisations that assist with refugee settlement, particularly through employment. www.ecre.org

HUMAN RIGHTS WATCH (HRW)
An international NGO that investigates and exposes human-rights violations and holds abusers accountable. It challenges governments to end abusive practices and respect the international law of human rights. www.hrw.org

INTERNATIONAL COMMITTEE OF THE RED CROSS
An impartial and independent organisation that directs and co-ordinates international relief activities and works to protect and provide assistance to victims of war and violence. Website: www.icrc.org

INTERNATIONAL INSTITUTE
An organisation that helps refugees and immigrants to gain independence by teaching them English, helping them find employment, gain access to social services and to generally adjust to the new way of life. www.intlinst.org

REFUGEES INTERNATIONAL
An organisation that serves refugees, displaced persons and other dispossessed people around the world through on-site field assessment missions. www.refintl.org